Best Maine Lobster Rolls

BEST MAINE
LOBSTER Rolls

Down East Books

Camden, Maine

Down East Books

Published by Down East Books

An imprint of The Rowman &
Littlefield Publishing Group, Inc.

4501 Forbes Blvd., Ste. 200

Lanham, MD 20706

www.rowman.com

Distributed by NATIONAL BOOK NETWORK

Copyright © 2018 The Rowman & Littlefield
Publishing Group, Inc.

Produced by Down East Custom Publishing Services
Project Editor Virginia M. Wright
Designer Miroslaw Jurek
Writers Brian Kevin, Joe Ricchio, Virginia M. Wright
Copyeditor Joe Anderson

British Library Cataloguing-in-Publication Information
available

**Library of Congress Cataloging-in-Publication Data
available**

ISBN 978-1-60893-995-4 (hardcover)
ISBN 978-1-60893-956-5 (e-book)

∞™ The paper used in this publication meets the
minimum requirements of American National Standard for
Information Sciences—Permanence of Paper for Printed
Library Materials, ANSI/NISO Z39.48-1992.

Photo credits: Cover: Bob's Clam Hut, Kristin Tieg · Title Page: Lobster Roll World Championship/Luke's Lobster, Douglas Merriam · Page 2: Libby's Market, Benjamin Williamson · Page 5: Quoddy Bay Lobster, Mark McCall · Page 6: Bayview Takeout, Mark McCall · Page 9: Douglas Merriam · Page 11: Nina Gallant · Page 13: Quoddy Bay Lobster, Mark McCall · Page 19: Lobster Roll World Championship/Bite Into Maine, Douglas Merriam · Page 23: Bayview Takeout, Mark McCall · Page 27: Lobster Roll World Championship/Freshies, Douglas Merriam · Pages 28–29: Shutterstock · Page 31: Quoddy Bay Lobster, Mark McCall · Page 34: Nina Gallant · Page 37: Mark McCall · Pages 38–39: Kristin Tieg · Pages 40–41: Jennifer Bakos, courtesy Bob's Clam Hut · Page 42: Daryl Getman, courtesy The Clam Shack · Page 43: Kristin Tieg · Pages 44–45: Zack Bowen, Knack Factory, courtesy Eventide Oyster Co. · Page 47: Kristin Tieg · Pages 48–49: Peter Bissell, courtesy Highroller Lobster · Pages 50–51: courtesy Luke's Lobster · Page 53: courtesy McLoons Lobster Shack · Pages 54–55: Mark McCall · Page 56: Kristin Tieg · Page 57: Nance Trueworthy · Page 59: Mark McCall · Pages 60–61: Eastport, Tyler Aldrich · Page 62: lobster, Shutterstock; Trenton Bridge Lobster Pound, Douglas Merriam · Page 63: Kristin Tieg · Page 65: Port Clyde, Benjamin Williamson · Page 66: Benjamin Williamson · Pages 68–69, 70: Kristin Tieg · Pages 72–73: Zack Bowen, Knack Factory, courtesy Eventide Oyster Co. · Page 75: Stacey Cramp, from Adventures in Comfort Food by Kerry Altiero and Katherine Gaudet, courtesy Page Street Publishing, Salem, MA · Page 79: Stacey Cramp · Page 80: Bob's Clam Hut, Kristin Tieg · Pages 82–83: Daryl Getman, courtesy the Clam Shack · Page 84–85: Jennifer Bakos, courtesy Bob's Clam Hut · Pages 86–87, 88–89: Lobster Shack at Two Lights, Benjamin Williamson · Page 91: Zack Bowen, Knack Factory, courtesy Eventide Oyster Co. · Pages 92–93: Highroller Lobster Co., Benjamin Williamson · Page 94: Lobster Roll World Championship/Bite Into Maine, Douglas Merriam · Page 95: Wharf Gallery & Grill, Mark McCall · Pages 96–97: Libby's Market, Benjamin Williamson · Pages 98–99: Five Islands, Benjamin Williamson · Page 100: courtesy McLoons Lobster Shack · Page 101: Luke's at Tenants Harbor, courtesy Luke's Lobster · Pages 102–103, 105: Wharf Gallery & Grill, Mark McCall · Pages 106–107, 109: Bayview Takeout, Mark McCall · Page 110–111: Wharf Gallery & Grill, Mark McCall · Page 112: Quoddy Bay Lobster, Mark McCall · Back cover: Nina Gallant

Contents

Introduction

"**THE LOBSTER ROLL,**" one travel writer gushes, "is as closely tied to Maine's identity as the crab cake is to Baltimore or the cheesesteak to Philly."

Seems like that's always been true, right? After all, Maine's beloved crustacean-on-a-bun inspires foodie pilgrimages, graces magazine covers, and prompts traffic jams in tourist season. But only a few decades back, the lobster roll was just another obscure seafood-shack menu item, no more renowned or emblematic of the Pine Tree State than, say, fried scallops or a bowl of steamers. Delicious? Of course! Nationally beloved? Hardly.

A hundred years ago, nobody had even heard of a lobster roll — not even in Maine. According to John F. Mariani's revered *Encyclopedia of American Food and Drink*, the phrase first appeared in print in *The New York Times* in 1937, and Mariani name-checks possible progenitor restaurants in Milford, Connecticut, and Long Island, New York (though our chats with lobster roll cognoscenti suggest there's more to the story).

For most of the 20th century, a smattering of New England restaurateurs hawked the dish in relative obscurity. Then, at the tail end of the '90s, a tiny restaurant in Manhattan, Pearl Oyster Bar, transformed the once-humble lobster roll into an object of culinary obsession — and a fleet of eager chefs, hyper-productive Maine fishermen, and savvy New York editors took over from there. By 2006, *Bon Appétit* had dubbed the lobster roll the dish of the year. It graced the cover of *Gourmet* in 2009. A 2010 *New York* magazine feature proclaimed its utter conquest of NYC, even as the lobster roll popped up on menus coast to coast, arguably usurping the classic shore dinner as Maine's quintessential dish.

Today, perhaps a century after its debut, young chefs and entrepreneurs are pushing the lobster roll's geographic and conceptual horizons. Put on your bib and enjoy the anything-but-simple story of a perfectly simple Maine treat.

CHAPTER 1

The Definitive Oral History of the Lobster Roll

It wasn't always Maine's marquee foodstuff.
How did a humble hot-dog bun crammed with the simplest of ingredients manage to attain rockstar status in the food world? We talked to the seafood slingers, chefs, glossy food-mag writers, and entrepreneurs who helped turn the unassuming lobster roll into a national phenomenon.

I. "It's Pretty Murky Back There."

DEBBIE GAGNON (co-owner/manager of Red's Eats in Wiscasset): There are so many stories. A million people will tell you a million different places where it originated.

REBECCA CHARLES (chef/owner at Pearl Oyster Bar in Greenwich Village, New York City): It's not like Buffalo wings, which came from that one place — I know of like three restaurants that claim to have invented the lobster roll.

BEN CONNIFF (president of the national Luke's Lobster chain): I'm pretty darned sure the first person was a lobsterman who had a bunch of left-over lobster and some bread. Whoever decided to put it on the menu first, I don't think you'll ever be able to definitively trace that.

MICHAEL STERN (co-author of the bestselling *Roadfood* guidebook): There is a pretty definitive origin story, actually. Oddly enough, the lobster roll was invented in Connecticut in 1929. What it was in those days — and what it remains to a large degree in Connecticut — is a hot lobster roll, which is hot lobster meat and butter in a bun. Whereas, to a lot of people in Connecticut, the kind of lobster roll you get as you travel more Down East is what they'd call a lobster salad roll, where it's cool and with mayonnaise. Before Harry Perry started serving it in Milford, Connecticut, I don't think there *were* lobster rolls.

SANDY OLIVER (New England food historian): Nobody ever invents anything. When it comes to food, practically everything we're eating has evolved from something that existed in the past. The lobster salad sand-

wich has been around since the 19th century, especially the last quarter or so. Those early salad dressings weren't always mayonnaise — they were often a vinegary, mustardy cream sauce. But lobster may have been tossed with that and maybe celery and served cold, and it was a major feature of weddings and other genteel gatherings.

SUSAN BAYLEY CLOUGH (co-owner of Bayley's Lobster Pound at Pine Point in Scarborough): In 1915, my great-grandfather was digging clams and catching lobsters in this area. When you get some lobsters with a broken claw or that restaurants or wholesalers wouldn't want, you have to figure out what to do with them. So my great-grandmother started cooking them in the kitchen of her house, on the same site we're on now, and selling them right out her window. At some point, my great-grandfather asked for a sandwich, and she put together mayonnaise and lobster meat. She put it on white bread, though, and cut the crusts off, because he didn't like crusts.

OLIVER: Probably the bright idea to stick it inside a bun was a commercial one. We started seeing what we know as a hot-dog roll in the 1910s. In New England, we have the famous split-top version — you can toast them, flatten them, open them up a bit, and dump your salad on top.

BAYLEY CLOUGH: In the years after they discovered the split-top hot-dog roll, my great-grandmother switched over, because of the crust issue for my great-grandfather. It's not like there's a lot of advertising material from 101 years ago, so it's hard to say, but between 1915 and 1917, it would had to have been. I keep telling my husband it's a war I'm winning by attrition. I defy somebody to come to me and tell me, "We've been here for 103 years, and let me tell you about my family."

MARIANNE LACROIX (marketing director at the Maine Lobster Marketing Collaborative): It'd be hard to disprove anyone who claims to be the first — it's pretty murky back there.

II. "What's a Lobster Roll?"

NANCY HARMON JENKINS (Camden-based food writer): My father, who was born in Machias in 1910, told me he didn't remember seeing lobster rolls before WWII, that it was a post-war thing. I was surprised at that, because I thought it had always been around.

SCOTT DESIMON (Cumberland native, special projects and deputy editor of *Bon Appétit* from 2011 to 2015): Most of that lobster-shack culture didn't spring up until the '50s, when people started traveling. My mom says, growing up, lobster rolls weren't really a thing you ate if you lived here — she didn't start having them until the '70s.

GAGNON: My dad bought [Red's Eats] in 1977. It was defunct, and I remember so many merchants going, "Why do you want to buy Red's?" Dad and I used to sit at the window, playing cribbage and waiting for customers. Then, in the late '80s maybe, Dad went to another restaurant and had a lobster roll, and it was frozen meat — it's like eating wet cardboard; I think it's a sin — and it had mayonnaise and celery and all this. He came back shaking his head and goes, "I'm going to make a lobster roll." After that, it was like a domino effect. People started talking about it and telling others, and people started coming.

BAYLEY CLOUGH: I started here when I was 12 years old, in 1978, but back then, and right up into the '90s, when people came in and saw "lobster rolls" on our sign, they didn't know what it was. You'd answer that question about 200 times a day. "What's a lobster roll?" About half thought it had something to do with an egg roll. It's funny because now, in the last 10 or 15 years, nobody asks that question anymore.

MICHAEL LANDGARTEN (owner of Bob's Clam Hut in Kittery): When I took over Bob's in 1986, on a summer day, we would do 60 or 70 [lobster rolls]. Now, some days I think we do 300. It's the biggest-selling single menu item.

STEVE KINGSTON (owner of The Clam Shack in Kennebunk): I remember selling 84 lobster rolls in a day was a record in my first year, 16 years ago. Our record now is 502. We feed way more people, but it just doesn't seem to be slowing down, and it seems like every restaurant in Maine has one now. Rebecca Charles gets a lot of credit for that — she was on the cutting edge of the casual oyster bar thing in New York City, before it became chic.

HARMON JENKINS: It was partly Rebecca Charles. It was partly Jasper White.

JASPER WHITE (chef/owner of Summer Shack in Boston, author of the cookbook *Lobster at Home*): I might have been the first chef to do a lobster roll on an upscale menu. In the '80s, I had a fine dining restaurant, Jasper's, and I introduced a lobster roll on our summer menu. I had to dress it up, which is kind of what I did with New England cooking back then. I did a saffron New England bun, homemade beet pickles, and homemade fancy potato chips.

It surprised me later when it became so popular in New York — and once it hit there, it just became a national craze.

III. "Oh, This Thing from Maine Is Now in New York."

CHARLES: I was in New York City cooking in the 1970s, and it was a drug-infested carnival ride. A few years of that and I was like, oh my god, I'm not going to make it to 30. So when mom bought a house in Kennebunk in 1979, I thought, why don't I just move up there? We had a long history of coming to Kennebunk — there are pictures of me at Kennebunk Beach at 11 months, lying on my stomach and smiling. I wound up working at the Whistling Oyster, and from there I went to the White Barn Inn and a little restaurant I opened called Café 74, which only lasted about a year.

I lived in Kennebunk until about '87, when I went back to the city. By 1996, I was sick of taking chef jobs for New York restaurant owners who didn't know anything about the restaurant business. I went to Napa to take a breather, and I read a guidebook on the plane about this place, Swan Oyster Depot in San Francisco. Right off the plane, I went, and they just had oysters and San Francisco–style seafood. Very simple, a bunch of guys working behind a counter, serving fish out the front window. I thought, oh my god, this is fantastic — we don't have anything like this in New York! I got back and started looking for a small space. I thought, they're doing San Francisco style — okay, I'll do New England style.

DESIMON: When I moved to New York in 1995, the only lobster roll I remember was kind of a fancy version at Grand Central Oyster Bar. Other

> "It's a sandwich that has to have store-bought mayonnaise. When I serve bouillabaisse, I'm making the mayo, but when I serve a lobster roll, it's Hellmann's."

than that, you couldn't find them. When Pearl Oyster Bar opened [in 1997], that was the first moment of, "Oh, this thing from Maine is now in New York."

LANDGARTEN: Rebecca Charles' whole schtick — it was more than schtick, it was the brilliant thing she did — was to elevate this fishermen's food, and she was brilliant enough not to overcomplicate things.

CHARLES: It was a very small space — it started out with 21 seats, bar and counter seating and one table that was bitterly fought over. I spent the longest time searching for buns and trying to get bakers to make them, then realized that the Pepperidge Farm bun I put my hot dog in is so much better than any of this, so I just went with that. And for me, it's a sandwich that has to have store-bought mayonnaise. When I serve a bouillabaisse, I'm making the mayonnaise, but when I serve a lobster roll, it's Hellmann's.

BARBARA FAIRCHILD (editor-in-chief of *Bon Appétit* from 2000 to 2011): For me, it's something that transports you to the place where you might have first had it in Maine — that's what I liked about Pearl, which is such a charming building on a charming street in charming Greenwich Village. You sit there and think, I almost *am* in Maine. All we're missing is the water outside.

CHARLES: It was about two weeks before I started to get attention, and reviewers singled out the lobster roll right away. I think the first person to write about us was Ed Levine [of *The New York Times*], and after he did, all hell broke loose. We had a magazine or a newspaper in once a week, and it snowballed.

IV. "And Then It Just Went Viral."

LANDGARTEN: This could be a myth at this point, but I'm pretty sure Rebecca Charles was on the cover of *Gourmet* or *Bon Appétit* or one of these with a lobster roll. After that, Martha Stewart jumped on, and everyone and their brother was making lobster rolls on television, and it's showing up in magazines. It became an icon of summertime.

KINGSTON: For us, the first real breakout one was *USA Today* in 2000. They did "50 Plates from 50 States" — they chose an iconic food and then a place. They chose a lobster roll, and they chose The Clam Shack.

GAGNON: Back in 1995, *CBS Sunday Morning*, with Tim Sample, that was the first national press that I remember. And then it just went viral — the Food Network, even Nippon Television in Japan.

KINGSTON: We were in a *Travel + Leisure* article in 2003 or 2004, and the interviewer said, "It'd be cool if you could get the makings of this thing and have them shipped to you." Well I said, we could do that. Lo and behold, she put in a sidebar like, "Get the makings for your Maine lobster roll from The Clam Shack!" I didn't even have a FedEx account. So subscribers get this magazine, the phone starts ringing, and I have a market manager saying, "Steve, I just got my third phone call for a lobster roll kit. What are these people talking about?" I went, "Oh shit! Are you kidding me? Take the order! Take the phone number!" Suddenly we were selling the Maine Lobster Roll Kit, and we just crushed it that first summer with orders, all from one article.

HARMON JENKINS: The key to the whole thing is New York because that's where the magazine editors are, and you can't get anything past them unless it's in New York — then it becomes a big deal. Then everybody in the country wants it.

RUTH REICHL (editor of *Gourmet* from 1999 to 2009): I wish I could tell you about the conversations that went into choosing a lobster roll for the cover of the magazine [in July of 2009]. I would like to think I never had that much hubris that I would think, "Yeah, we're going to make X dish famous." Certainly, at *Gourmet*, we wouldn't say of a particular dish, you know, "Tikka masala needs to be famous!"

FAIRCHILD: But so many people come to New York as a tourist destination that once a dish is sort of on the "must-have list," people come from all over to eat it, then they go home and tell their friends. Hence the Cronut [a croissant-doughnut hybrid that New Yorkers have lined up for since 2013]. Once the word gets out, a dish spreads its tentacles all across the country: the pastrami sandwich at Carnegie Deli, the Cronut, the Pearl Oyster Bar lobster roll.

V. "Suddenly, They Were All Over the Place."

REICHL: When Rebecca Charles opened up Pearl, nobody was eating lobster rolls. Then suddenly, they were all over the place. And certainly the fact that lobsters got cheap was a big factor in the growing popularity of it.

LACROIX: Historically, [Maine lobstermen] were catching 20–25 million pounds a year, and that started going up. In the early 2000s, you're looking at maybe 60 million pounds coming in. There's a lot of speculation

> "The key to the whole thing is New York because that's where the magazine editors are, and you can't get anything past them unless it's in New York — then it becomes a big deal."

> ### "It was chef-y chefs who'd never left New York City. They were over-garnishing and using so much lobster that they no longer understood the concept."

as to why: the industry has been managing the resource since the 1800s, so there are a lot of sustainability measures in place. Cod were overfished and the cod fishery went down — those were considered a predator, so that's a factor. Processing was also becoming more popular. Back in the '90s, lobster was more of a white-tablecloth item, and surf and turf — a piece of steak and a lobster tail — was big. And it was sort of like, "All right, now what are we going to do with all this claw and knuckle meat?"

DESIMON: I'm guessing [New York restaurants] use quite a bit of picked lobster meat, because almost no one in a New York kitchen — other than, say, Pearl — is steaming the lobsters and picking the meat themselves.

CHARLES: That's what's wrong with most lobster rolls. We get all of the lobster into that tiny restaurant to the tune of 1,500 pounds a week, and we steam it all in-house, throw it into ice-water baths. We break it down, we pick it, we cut it. We have a very specific methodology.

It was only a couple of months before other restaurateurs were coming with cameras and pads, trying to determine what was in the Pearl lobster roll. I've learned the hard way that people can copy you right down to the exact way you do everything, and there's not a lot you can do about it.

FROM *THE NEW YORK TIMES*: "Do not invite Rebecca Charles and Mary Redding to the same clambake. They opened the snug but sparkling Pearl Oyster Bar together in Greenwich Village in 1997, but bitterly dissolved their partnership, with Ms. Charles retaining sole ownership of Pearl. Ms. Redding then opened her own place, Mary's Fish Camp, a few blocks away, offering virtually the same menu of New England–inspired seafood." ("A Rivalry Fought Out in Dueling Lobster Rolls," by Eric Asimov; May 23, 2001)

"The owner and chef of a Greenwich Village seafood restaurant has

settled the lawsuit she brought against her former sous-chef after he opened a restaurant that she said was a 'total plagiarism' of her own. The chef, Rebecca Charles of Pearl Oyster Bar, had accused her former assistant, Edward McFarland, of copying 'each and every element' of her restaurant." ("Chef's Lawsuit Against a Former Assistant Is Settled Out of Court," by Pete Wells; April 19, 2008)

BEN SARGENT (aka "Dr. Klaw" of Brooklyn's short-lived Underground Lobster Pound, former restaurateur, host of the Cooking Channel's *Hook, Line & Dinner* from 2011 to 2013): What started to happen was that people were just riffing off of Rebecca Charles. And I was like, no! Go on a trip to Maine, because even *hers* is her own version! It was chef-y chefs who'd never left New York City. They were over-garnishing, and they were putting so much lobster in the roll that they no longer understood the concept, because the point is the ratio of buttery toasted bun to succulent lobster.

So I woke up one day [in early 2010] and was like, I'm going to make a lobster roll in my Brooklyn apartment and show these guys what a lobster roll is all about. It was all run by text message, all word-of-mouth. I'd operate from dark until about 1 in the morning. I had to operate under the name "Dr. Klaw" because I needed an alias. And it worked, for a while, which was crazy. I was having people down to my teeny tiny apartment and selling 250 lobster rolls a night [with Maine-sourced lobster].

I got kind of a slap on the wrist from the fire department — they said I had enough propane in my apartment to blow up a city block — and eventually, the health department sent a notice to me and to my landlord: "Benjamin F.W. Sargent, dba 'The Lobster Pusher Man,' operating as 'Dr. Klaw.'" They threatened me with jail time.

MICHAEL CIMARUSTI (chef/owner at Providence, Connie and Ted's, and Cape Seafood & Provisions in Los Angeles): Maybe there were places in LA that did lobster rolls every once in a while, but only five or six years ago did you start seeing them here more often. At Connie and Ted's [opened in 2013], we'll get anywhere between 700 and 900 pounds of whole lobster throughout the week, specifically for the lobster roll. It can account for as much as 20 percent of the entrée sales in any given day.

SABIN LOMAC (Scarborough native, co-founder and co-owner of the national, Los Angeles–based Cousins Maine Lobster chain of food trucks): When we first started doing this [in 2012], we weren't sure that people in LA even knew what a lobster roll was.

JIM TSELIKIS (Cape Elizabeth native, co-founder and co-owner of Cousins Maine Lobster): We thought about doing Italian sandwiches, but we kept coming back to lobster, because that's our identity and our tradition. It was going to be a passion project, maybe break even. Then we had lines 50 people deep on day one, and [ABC's reality TV show] *Shark Tank* reached out to us the night before we'd even served a roll. ["Shark" Barbara Corcoran, of the show's investor panel, bought 15% of the company for $55,000.]

LOMAC: We were astounded by how many people were driving 30, 40, 50 miles for a lobster roll. We had a guy drive from Phoenix one time. We just opened in San Antonio [the company's 13th city and 19th truck], and there were people there, especially wayward New Englanders, who were genuinely grateful.

LUKE HOLDEN (Cape Elizabeth native, founder and CEO of the national Luke's Lobster chain): My father had the very first lobster-processing

> **"I had to operate under the alias 'Dr. Klaw.' I was having people down to my teeny tiny apartment and selling 250 lobster rolls a night."**

license in the state of Maine, 30-plus years ago, so that was the business I grew up in, whether it was on the docks or the processing facility. I wanted to be on the water, so I got a job as a sternman, right in Kettle Cove in Cape Elizabeth. I learned how to fish there.

We opened in 2009, building on the lobster roll's momentum in NYC. The question was, why are all these incredible chefs screwing this thing up so badly? We cut out the middleman and brought the product to urban environments in a fast-casual fare that didn't exist. We're at 26 locations now. We're comfortable growing five to eight shacks a year in the next five to seven years, which puts us hopefully somewhere around 75 shacks domestically, across the U.S.

LACROIX: These guys [Luke's and Cousins] are doing an amazing job. Both of them are also selling a story, which I think people really like right now, to know where their food is coming from and the story behind it.

JANE STERN (co-author of *Roadfood*): Can I be a contrarian? We've spent the better part of four decades preaching that the glory of American food done correctly is not just food on a plate but the ambience and gestalt. How anyone can replicate sitting on the end of a pier in Maine — with the gray Atlantic waters splashing against the wooden pillars and the salty air and the Down East accents — to eating it out of a truck in Des Moines is ridiculous to me.

VI. "Now Everybody Has to Differentiate Their Lobster Roll with What They Do That's Special."

BAYLEY CLOUGH: Going back to the 1970s, when people came in for lob-

ster rolls and brought friends from out of state, they would talk about it like this special thing they couldn't get anywhere else. "I couldn't wait to get back to Maine to get a lobster roll!" We don't have that anymore because you can get a lobster roll anywhere in the country — they have them at McDonald's, for goodness sake. So now everybody has to differentiate their lobster roll with what they do that's special.

KARL SUTTON (co-owner of Bite Into Maine food truck at Fort Williams in Cape Elizabeth): We were genuinely surprised [before opening in 2011] that everyone just used the Maine style, with some mayo, and there didn't seem to be a lot of variation. We were like, what are we missing? So we did some tastings and experiments with different flavor combinations that we thought paired well with the lobster, and that became the impetus and inspiration to open a food truck [which now serves curry-, chipotle-, and wasabi-style rolls, alongside the classics]. Sarah Sutton (co-owner of Bite Into Maine): We definitely sell more

*
For brevity and clarity, some portions of these quotes have been condensed.

Split-Top Bun

Side-Split Bun

●—**TRADITIONAL**————————————————

Mayo

Butter

Lettuce

Celery

traditional ones, but in the beginning, we were on the news, and then all of a sudden, we started getting these really old Mainers who were like, "I want a curry lobster roll!" because the TV reporter said they were good.

BAXTER KEY (co-founder/co-owner of The Highroller Lobster Co. food cart in Portland): We serve a lot of first-timers, people on vacation doing the beer circuit here, and they're like, "I've never had a lobster roll. How should I do it?" I'll say, I like it with bacon and jalapeño mayo. And they're always stoked about it.

ANDY GERRY (co-founder/co-owner of The Highroller): We knew at first people would be skeptical because we were messing with a classic.

KEY: There are definitely people with their opinions. We'll post a picture with, like, avocado and lime mayo, and people are like, "What are you doing?! You can't even taste the lobster!" in the comments section.

Round Roll

Brioche Bun

Puff Pastry

OUTLANDISH!

Chives

Wasabi/Curry/Chipotle

Avocado

Bacon

> **"We started getting these really old Mainers saying, 'I want a curry lobster roll' because the TV reporter said they were good."**

FAIRCHILD: It's one of those things like a well-made burger or club sandwich, those kinds of iconic dishes that never go out of style but also can adapt to modern eating. I daresay somewhere in this country, there's probably a lobster roll that has some kind of Asian seasoning or maybe some kind of South American or Latin seasoning. And it doesn't suffer. It's enhanced by reinterpretation, and I think that's why it endures.

JANE STERN: I think lobster rolls are totally minimalist cuisine. I remember watching Gordon Ramsay on TV about a year ago, showing how to make a lobster roll. It was a complete nightmare, because he had all this weird seasoning in it — thyme and I don't know what else. He wanted to make it interesting and chef-ish, but the best lobster roll depends only on the perfection of the lobster, how recently it was caught, how good it is — then butter and a roll.

CIMARUSTI: It's got to just be an exercise in purity.

CHARLES: When you elevate something, for me, you have to be careful not to take it somewhere else: somebody puts seaweed in it, someone else puts tarragon in it. You just — you can't do that. You have to keep it pure. Most people's biggest complaint about my lobster roll is that it's got too much mayonnaise. Well, I love mayonnaise, and I don't trust people who don't.

KINGSTON: I actually like those places that do some funky stuff. Questions about our round rolls used to really bother me — fortunately for us, the reputation of the product outgrew the skepticism.

WHITE: It's so hard to be a young chef now, because you just have to come up

with nonsense to get noticed. I did one change: some of the old classic lobster rolls have celery, but instead I do a small amount of chives in the mayonnaise, and cucumbers, which give it that little bit of crunch and texture.

DESIMON: All you need is butter, a split-top hot-dog bun, a lobster, and mayonnaise. And if you want a little bit of celery or something, go for it. You shouldn't. But whatever, you can.

SARGENT: If you put lettuce anywhere near my f*cking lobster roll, I'll just give it back.

LOMAC: If you're serving a roll on a baguette or brioche — I think at some point throughout my journeys in LA I've seen them on a puff pastry — it might look beautiful, but for me, it just doesn't have that tradition behind it.

OLIVER: Foods on the gimmicky side, they're not going to last. Like a Cronut? Oh, please. There's all kinds of garbage like that out there, and it dies its own natural death, and we should be grateful. The more a dish relates to the larger culture, if it's descended from a long family line of something, the more it's going to endure.

KINGSTON: People thought lobster mac and cheese was going to be the next chowder, but while you certainly see it on menus, it's not classic, because it's still not as pure. A lobster roll lets you taste the pureness of real lobster without going too crazy.

WHITE: Lobster mashed potatoes? Come on. Macaroni and cheese with lobster? It might be the best way you can eat macaroni and cheese, but it's got to be one of the worst ways you can eat lobster. To me, it's all about flavor, texture, aroma. Look at the great classic dishes, like bouillabaisse — it reached perfection 100 years ago. There's really not much to do with it. In the end, the dishes that last are the ones that have incredible flavor — which is probably why the hamburger has lasted through all kinds of bastardizations and fast-food garbage.

LANDGARTEN: You can't argue with the downright deliciousness of the lobster roll. Whether or not you get it hot with butter, you still have the hot butter carmelization on the roll, so the butter flavor is there. You get the fresh meat, you get the pop with the outer skin giving way to the inside, a burst of salty yummy flavor. It's just tremendous.

REICHL: It's our dish. Atlantic lobsters are an iconic American food, and it makes sense we would democratize this thing that in almost all the rest of the world is a luxury food by putting it on a hot-dog bun with a lot of mayonnaise — that we would bring it down to ballpark level. The lobster roll makes more sense to me as an icon of American food than a hamburger. I mean "hamburger" isn't even an American word. We didn't invent it. Lobster rolls are really ours.

This story originally ran in the August 2016 issue of Down East *magazine.*

CHAPTER 2

Masters
of the Roll

THERE ARE HUNDREDS of places in Maine that serve great lobster rolls, but only a few are icons. Each has acquired superstar status for reasons as distinctive as the eatery itself. Often it's the setting: a takeout stand perched on the rocky shore that you swear must be the most beautiful place in the world to eat a simple sandwich — until you visit the next one. Sometimes it's the history: an eatery with roots so deep that no visit to the village counts if you haven't partaken of a meal there. A few are famous for being famous: somewhere along the line, a prominent food writer or morning show host — no one remembers who or when — sang the place's praises and started a never-ending avalanche of positive publicity and long lines. There's a new breed of lobster roll influencers too: they are the chefs who reinvented a classic sandwich and did it so well that Mainers, notorious for their reticence to change, are among the biggest fans.

Bayview Takeout

42 Bayview Dr., Beals

207-497-3301 . facebook.com/bestlobsterrollsandseafoodinmaine

When *USA Today* readers voted Bayview Takeout's lobster roll as the country's best in 2016, no one was more surprised than owner Frank Alley. "It shocked me," says Alley, who started Bayview in 2007 "with a George Foreman Grill, a Walmart fryer, hopes and dreams, and not much else." He suspects his neighbors may have been the extra-enthusiastic voters who put Bayview's lobster roll in *USA Today*'s number-one spot.

Not that the lobster roll didn't deserve to be there. It's just that Beals, population 500, is well off the beaten tourist track. Pleasure boats are rare in the working harbor it shares with Jonesport. Souvenir shops and cute boutiques are rarer. Other than the stunning Great Wass Island Preserve off Beals' southern tip, there's little to lure vacationers from Route 1, 15 miles to the north.

Or, rather, there *was* little. Now, thanks to the *USA Today* poll, people flock to Beals especially for Bayview Takeout's lobster roll, a buttered and toasted split-top bun that's so overflowing with big chunks of lobster meat, you're best off attacking it with a fork rather than holding it in your hands. Alley and his wife, Sarah, dress their meat generously with Hellmann's and top each roll with a whole claw. The menu also includes hamburgers, fried clams, and the locals' favorite, fried haddock sandwiches.

Alley buys his lobsters from Look Lobster Company, across the bridge in Jonesport, which claims to be the country's first lobster dealer, dating back to 1910. Look in turn buys its lobsters from local lobstermen, who include Alley's brother and father. A propensity to seasickness keeps Alley from fishing himself, but he says with a chuckle, "I bet I've shelled a lot more lobsters than they have."

The Elements

The Bun: a buttered and grilled split-top roll

The Meat: fresh lobster from local lobstermen

The Mix: Hellmann's

The Scene: a perch overlooking the Jonesport-Beals lobsterboat-filled harbor

MASTERS *– of the –* **ROLL**

Bite Into Maine

Food Truck: Fort Williams Park, Cape Elizabeth. Allagash Brewing Co.: 50 Industrial Way, Portland. The Commissary: 185 U.S. Rte. 1, Scarborough. 207-289-6142. biteintomaine.com

With its exotically spiced sandwiches, the Bite Into Maine food truck at Fort Williams Park got a ton of favorable press right out of the gate in 2011, but Sarah and Karl Sutton didn't realize they'd joined the pantheon of the country's best lobster rolls until they were a few seasons into the gig. "People were coming to the food truck just for us, not knowing there was a lighthouse there," Sarah says. "We'd say, 'Oh, yeah, that's Portland Head Light. It's one of the most photographed lighthouses in the world.'"

The location, in fact, is partly what inspired the Suttons to build a better lobster roll. "This is one of the most beautiful places in the world," Sarah says, "and we wanted to elevate that experience with a lobster roll that was of the same caliber."

They also credit their own ignorance. Native Minnesotans, they weren't aware how deeply entrenched attitudes about authentic lobster rolls were. "We couldn't understand why there was no variety," Sarah says. "You pretty much got it one way and that was it."

To develop their menu, they invited friends to their home for a taste test and landed on the three flavored mayos that immediately set their lobster rolls apart — wasabi, smoky chipotle, and yellow Indian curry. They also settled on two classic iterations — Maine-style (mayo and chives) and Connecticut-style (warm butter) — as well as Sarah's favorite, the Picnic, which has coleslaw, drawn butter, and celery salt.

Bite Into Maine has since expanded to two other locations — a seasonal Airstream at Allagash Brewing and a year-round shop in Scarborough. "We're so lucky," Sarah says. "Never in a million years would I have imagined that we'd be in the same conversation as places like Red's Eats and The Clam Shack."

The Elements

The Bun: a grilled, locally baked, split-top roll

The Meat: fresh lobster from local purveyors

The Mix: wasabi mayo; smoky chipotle mayo; yellow Indian curry mayo; mayo and chives; melted butter; or coleslaw, butter, and celery salt

The Scene: three locations, but it's hard to beat the crashing waves and classic lighthouse at Fort Williams Park

Bob's Clam Hut

315 U.S. Rte. 1, Kittery
207-439-4233. bobsclamhut.com

By the time he graduated from Bowdoin College in 1980, Michael Landgarten had developed a fondness for classic road food — burgers, fish sandwiches, French fries, chocolate milkshakes, and the like. He even maintained a chalkboard rating system of all the joints he visited. "I was Zagats," he says with a chuckle, "before there was a Zagats." It didn't occur to him that he might like to own a restaurant though. He was going to be an artist, or a musician, or a lawyer, or . . . okay, he admits, "I was pretty lost."

A few years later, Landgarten — 26, a new dad, and still pretty lost — landed on the idea of owning a business. A friend pointed him to Bob's Clam Hut, where owner Bob Kraft was getting set to retire. "It was like being in a Norman Rockwell painting — it was so genuine," Landgarten says. He worked alongside the Kraft family for several weeks before they agreed to sell. "I wanted them to teach me how to be like that."

Opened in 1956, Bob's Clam Hut was, as its name suggests, famous for its fried clams, which Kraft dredged simply in flour — no egg wash and no breading to bulk them up so fewer were needed to fill a plate. "Bob didn't want to hide the flavor," Landgarten says. "He believed in the fabulous, briny taste of the clam, and he was willing to put more on the plate to keep it."

Kraft took the same approach with his finger-size lobster rolls, mixing the meat with just touch of Hellmann's so the rich lobster flavor shone through. Landgarten hasn't changed a thing, except the size — they're full sandwiches now, by customer demand (lobster rolls now outsell clams), with lightly dressed meat mounding a good inch or more above the buns. "They're much in the spirit of what Bob did with the clams," says Landgarten, now a restaurant mogul (by Maine standards) with two other Kittery eateries, Robert's Maine Grill and Lil's Café. "We're ultra-fussy about our lobster meat — it's the star."

The Elements

The Bun: lightly buttered split-top, toasted on both sides

The Meat: cooked in seawater, shucked, and delivered by a Kittery seafood processor

The Mix: a touch of Hellmann's

The Scene: smack in a busy retail section of Rte. 1, Bob's is decorated with historic photos, buoys and fish, and life-size cut-outs of the *Gilligan's Island* cast and of the late Lillian Mangos, a longtime window server, asking "What'll ya have?"

The Clam Shack

2 Western Ave., Kennebunk
207-967-3321 . theclamshack.net

If The Clam Shack got any closer to the Kennebunk River, it'd fall in. The little white shanty anchors the east end of the Mathew J. Lanigan Bridge, serving as a sort of welcome sign for Kennebunk and Kennebunkport alike since 1968. The charming location — and some of the plumpest, sweetest fried clams you'll ever taste — have made the place a Maine icon. These days, though, the Clam Shack is equally well known for its distinctive round lobster roll. It's so famous, in fact, the famous come looking for it: Teri Hatcher, Patrick Dempsey, Bobby Orr, Jim Nance, and Al Roker, to name a few. It's also a consistent fan favorite of New York's Lobster Roll Rumble.

"It all comes down to fresh-picked meat," says owner Steve Kingston. "We start picking at 10 A.M., and we'll keep going until 8 or 9. What we pick goes into that evening's sandwiches and the next day's lunch, so it's super, super fresh."

The Clam Shack gets its lobsters, cooked in seawater, from its next-door seafood market, and the crew picks 300–400 pounds of lobster meat on a slow day; three times that on a summer Saturday, when people will wait in line for more than an hour for a griddled roll filled with 5½ ounces of meat. Each roll has at least some portion of an entire one-pound lobster — tail, claw, and what Kingston calls "the sweetest part," the knuckles.

Equally important as the fresh seafood is The Clam Shack's round yeast bun, delivered six days a week by Reilly's Bakery in Biddeford. "It's a beautiful yeast white roll," Kingston says. "It's really soft, and it takes the butter beautifully. It tastes so much better than a standard white-bread roll." To those who would balk at this tradition-breaking bun, Kingston says, "Close your eyes and take a bite; it will beat any sandwich out there."

The Elements

The Bun: a locally baked round yeast roll

The Meat: 5½ ounces from a lobster that was very likely caught that morning off Cape Porpoise

The Mix: a little mayo, a little drizzled butter, or both

The Scene: perched on a bridge over the Kennebunk River, between Kennebunk's Lower Village and Kennebunkport's Dock Square

GUESTCHECK™

504189

7/22

APPT-SOUP/SAL-ENTREE-VEG/POT-DESSERT-BEV

1 Lobster Roll
mayo + Butter

1 Fries + Slaw

Tax
Total

Thank You

www.nationalchecking.com

MADE IN THE U.S.A.

Receipt

Date   Amount   Guests   50418

Eventide Oyster Co.

86 Middle St., Portland
207-774-8538. eventideoysterco.com

Eventide is the restaurant embodiment of what's happened to Portland in recent years: it's cool, romantic, sophisticated, and totally come-as-you-are. Chef Mike Wiley insists that he and his co-owners, chef Andrew Taylor and general manager Arlin Smith, were not prescient when they wed their love for Maine with their love for crudos just as Portland's I-wear-duck-boots-and-flannel-shirts-to-my-locally-sourced-dinner zeitgeist was rising. "We kind of stumbled into it backwards," he says.

Eventide, and its now-legendary lobster roll, quickly attracted local and national attention, including a spot on *Food & Wine* magazine's Best New Restaurants list that year. In 2016, *Condé Nast Traveler* proclaimed Eventide one of the world's best restaurants, and in 2017, Wiley and Taylor won the James Beard Award for Best Chef: Northeast (they were nominees in 2015 and 2016).

Eventide was conceived to be the casual, inexpensive sister of elegant Hugo's, which Wiley and company purchased in 2012. With picnic tables and an ice-filled, 1,500-pound granite basin showcasing fresh, raw oysters — another serendipitous choice, as oyster farming was just blossoming in Maine — Eventide is a stylish riff on the classic seafood shack.

"To open a restaurant referencing Maine so closely, you can't not have a lobster roll," Wiley says. "But lobster rolls in Maine are kind of like barbecue in South Carolina: people have strong feelings about what's authentic, and they want you to pick a team. Rather than pick a team, we made our own team."

Their "team" is an adaptation of a favorite Hugo's bar snack, the steamed pork bun: freshly picked lobster meat is tossed in a brown-butter-and-chives vinaigrette and stuffed into a soft, moist, steamed Asian-style bun. It's simple, surprising, and utterly delicious — a high-brow/low-brow treat, just like Eventide itself.

The Elements

The Bun: split-top, Asian-style steamed bun

The Meat: fresh, locally caught lobster

The Mix: a dressing of brown butter, lemon, and chives

The Scene: small, casual oyster bar in Portland's historic Old Port

MASTERS
– of the –
ROLL

Greet's Eats

West Main St., Vinalhaven
207-863-2057. facebook.com/greetseats

Fifteen miles off the coast of Rockland, Vinalhaven island lies among Maine's richest lobstering grounds. No wonder it produces an outstanding lobster roll.

You'll find it a short walk from the state ferry terminal at Greet's Eats, Greta McCarthy's food truck perched on the edge of Carvers Harbor. When McCarthy is running low on lobster, she simply opens the back door and calls out to her next-door neighbor, the Vinalhaven Fisherman's Coop. A skiff soon pulls up to offload a fresh catch at her feet.

Greta, a seventh-generation islander, has lobstering in her blood. Her husband, son, and son-in-law fish. So did her father and grandfather. But Greta cooks. She's worked in the kitchen for as long as she can remember, serving as a cook for summer people.

Several years ago, when prices for lobster hit a record low, Greta ventured out on her own to generate some extra income. She set up a lunch cart and began selling hot dogs, hamburgers, and lobster rolls. Greta attributes much of her early success to interest generated by the construction of three wind turbines on Vinalhaven that summer. "Everyone would come gawk at the big pieces being carried in," she says.

What kept people coming back, however, was her lobster roll.

She has since swapped out the hot-dog cart for a red food truck she found in *Uncle Henry's*. It is always parked in the same spot, overlooking Carvers Harbor, where lobsterboat sterns are stacked high with traps and gulls circle overhead.

Each Greet's Eats roll is filled with fresh, sweet lobster that's been cooked in salt water and chopped into small pieces and bound by a light dressing of mayo and Miracle Whip. Pair it with an order of Greta's Fancy Fries (seasoned with parmesan, garlic powder, and pepper), and you have a meal that's well worth the hour-long ferry ride from Rockland.

The Elements

The Bun: lightly buttered, toasted on both sides

The Meat: freshly caught from Penobscot Bay and cooked in salt water

The Mix: a mixture of two parts mayo to one part Miracle Whip, well seasoned with pepper

The Scene: lobsterboats, ferry traffic — about as Maine as it gets

Highroller Lobster Co.

Restaurant: 104 Exchange St., Portland. 207-536-1623
Food cart: Commercial St. at Pearl. highrollerlobster.com

In 2015, Baxter Key and Andy Gerry opened one of Maine's smallest and most creative lobster roll kitchens. Working at a waist-high, stainless-steel grill cart on the Portland waterfront, the best friends since high school served sandwiches that broke the unwritten rule of Maine lobster roll construction (lobster, mayo, a griddled split-top roll, and nothing, absolutely nothing, else). "We knew we'd have to offer plain mayo," Key says, "but we also decided to switch it up and make it interesting for people from Maine like us."

Key and Gerry pumped up the flavor, mixing their lobster with mayo that had been spiked with fresh lime juice and zest, jalapeños, and roasted red peppers, as well as with ghee, the nutty-tasting clarified butter used in Indian cooking. Instead of factory-bakery rolls, they ordered split-top brioches baked just for them by South Portland restaurant One Fifty Ate.

Key and Gerry's hunch proved right: Mainers do have more adventurous palates than the plain-Yankee stereotype suggests. Locals clamored for their exotic riffs, while the tourists favored the traditional iterations. The sandwiches sold so briskly that within three years, the Highroller boys had partnered with Pete Bissell, of Bissell Brothers brewery, to open a year-round brick-and-mortar location in the Old Port. There, lobster rolls are the number-one-selling item (the customer favorite is lime mayo), followed closely by lobster grilled cheese on English-muffin bread, and a lobster taco with a cheese-crisp shell. The latter is a food-cart creation inspired by the tasty bits of Jarlsberg and cheddar that had oozed out of the grilled cheese sandwich to sizzle on the griddle. Key and Gerry now sprinkle cheese on the grill deliberately, letting it melt into big discs that they fold over, stuff with lobster and lettuce, and drizzle with flavored mayonnaise. Come to think of it, it looks rather like a variation on the lobster roll, perhaps the most ingenious one yet.

The Elements

The Bun: a locally baked, split-top brioche, lightly buttered, grilled on both sides

The Meat: supplied by Portland-based Ready Seafood

The Mix: drizzles of lime mayo, jalapeño mayo, or red-pepper mayo; ghee; old-school mayo; and melted butter

The Scene: Old Port pub with big selection of craft brews. Seasonal cart on waterfront Commercial St.

Luke's at Tenants Harbor

12 Commercial St., St. George. 207-691-3020. lukeslobster.com

Luke Holden has turned the Maine-brand-meets-national-success story on its head. Instead of launching Luke's Lobster in his native state, Holden opened his first seafood shack in lobster-roll-deprived New York City in 2009, where it was an immediate hit. Seven years, eight cities, and 18 restaurants later, Holden brought Luke's home, opening in a former fish market in Tenants Harbor. Nothing about the weathered shanty says "national chain." You would think Luke's had been sitting on Millers Wharf for decades.

Holden had no experience in running a restaurant when he opened his first Luke's Lobster, but he did know lobsters. He grew up in Cape Elizabeth, where his dad was a lobster processor and fisherman; as a teenager, Holden worked as a sternman. The family lived near the venerable Lobster Shack at Two Lights, which Holden credits (along with his mom) for his unfussy approach to seafood.

That's what he was yearning when, as a Wall Street investment banker just two years out of college, he dreamed up the idea of opening a lobster shack in Manhattan. "I was sitting at my desk on a warm, sunny July afternoon, and I was missing home," he recalls. But New York chefs seemed compelled to fancy up their expensive lobster rolls with additions like celery, cucumbers, Dijon, and tarragon. So Holden decided to offer a fresh taste of home: a split-top bun stuffed with fresh lobster mixed with a small amount of lightly seasoned mayonnaise.

Since the beginning, Holden has purchased exclusively from Maine fishermen. In 2012, he and his brother Bryan opened Cape Seafood, a processing plant in Saco, to supply the growing restaurant chain. With Luke's at Tenants Harbor, he's notched up his support for Maine fisheries: Half the restaurant's profits go to the Tenants Harbor Fisherman's Co-op, and Cape Seafood is the guaranteed buyer of every lobster hauled by the co-op's 20 members. It may be link number 19 in the Luke's Lobster chain, but one senses it's number one in Luke Holden's heart.

The Elements

The Bun: New England–style, split-top roll

The Meat: purchased from the Tenants Harbor Fisherman's Co-op and processed in Saco

The Mix: a little mayo and a light sprinkling of secret seasoning

The Scene: easy-going seafood shack with seating indoors and outdoors on the wharf. A small bar serves Maine microbrews, wine, and Maine-distilled liquors

MASTERS
- of the -
ROLL

McLoons Lobster Shack

315 Island Rd., South Thomaston. 207-593-1382. mcloonslobster.com

No storage tanks for McLoons' lobsters! The crustaceans are held in floating crates in the bay just off McLoons Wharf and plucked from the seawater just before they're cooked. That's why the meat in McLoons lobster rolls is so sweet, succulent, and tender.

Thanks to the rolls, the tidy red takeout shack on Spruce Head Island has developed a large loyal following since it opened in 2012. The setting, on a secluded cove with views of spruce-covered islands and stunning sunsets, doesn't hurt, either. McLoons is at the end of a quiet road with not much on it besides homes and a lobster dealer, so people tend to either stumble on it while exploring the area or they get sent there by a friend who discovered it that way.

McLoons Wharf, one of the area's oldest lobster-buying stations, is owned by the Douty family, who also owns Douty Brothers Seafood, a wholesale business in Portland, and Lusty Lobster, a retail store in New Jersey. Bree Douty manages the lobster shack with a nod to both tradition and contemporary tastes. Simple preparations allow fresh, local ingredients to shine. There's no fryolator, for example, so instead of fried clams, there are littlenecks, roasted to smoky deliciousness. Everything is house-made, from the garlic herb butter served with those clams to the rich and chunky lobster stew to the pies, filled with seasonal berries and fruits. Fresh herbs — thyme, rosemary, parsley, and mint — grow in window boxes, and diners are invited to help themselves should they want to add a personal touch to their meal.

If you happen to order the lobster roll, our suggestion is leave the herbs for another day. The fresh meat itself is unadorned, and for good reason: it's pretty much perfect.

The Elements

The Bun: buttered, toasted split-top roll

The Meat: kept in seawater until it's ready for the pot, the lobsters are as fresh as it gets

The Mix: mayo, if you want it, is brushed lightly on the inside of the bun; butter is served on the side

The Scene: island-dotted Seal Harbor, and lobsterboats bringing in catches a stone's throw from your picnic table

Quoddy Bay Lobster

7 Sea St., Eastport. 207-853-6640.

It's easy to find a lobster shack with spectacular ocean views in Maine, but only one doubles as a whale watch: that's Quoddy Bay Lobster, with front-row seats on Friar Roads, the passage between Eastport and Campobello Island. There, minke, finback, and humpback whales are frequently seen surfacing in July and August.

As breathtaking as they are, though, the whales are not what bring people to Quoddy Bay Lobster. The lobster rolls do.

Quoddy Bay Lobster is the serendipitous spin-off of a wholesale lobster business owned by the Griffin family — brothers Mike, Jeff, and Dale, and Dale's son, Brent, all fishermen. The business is located just downhill from Eastport's only motel, whose guests regularly popped in to inquire about buying lobsters. To serve them, the Griffins decided to opened a retail store in 2011, learning during the inspection that their permit would allow them to have a small lunch counter. They brought in a countertop griddle — the kind you pull out of the cupboard for Sunday brunch guests — and Dale's wife, Shelley, and Brent's wife, Sara, spent that first season minding the store and filling toasted rolls with the fresh lobster and crab that a dozen or so fishermen deliver to Quoddy Bay every day. The following year, they added fish chowder to their limited menu. "We made it on Thursday, and if it lasted through the weekend, great, and if it didn't, great," Sara recalls, "Either way, we didn't make another chowder until the next Thursday."

Food service, in other words, was very much "by the way," but that changed quickly as customer demand rose. These days, the restaurant is Quoddy Bay Lobster's main event in summer, with 20-odd employees cooking and serving nearly 30 different menu items. The lobster roll is the runaway favorite in three sizes: the junior with about 2 ounces of lobster meat, the regular with 4 ounces, and the jumbo, so big at 8 ounces it requires an oversized 8-inch-long bun.

The Elements

The Bun: buttered, and griddled, split-top hot-dog rolls

The Meat: lobster, caught and delivered to Quoddy Bay's dock, then cooked and picked usually within 24 hours

The Mix: mayo, Miracle Whip, drawn butter, or any combination of the three, mixed lightly or generously into the meat or served on the side

The Scene: Eastport's working waterfront, with lobsterboats going and coming and whales surfacing in Friar Roads

Red's Eats

41 Water St., Wiscasset
207-882-6128 . redseatsmaine.com

Gregarious and enormously funny, Al Gagnon didn't found Red's Eats, but he put the tiny eatery — and some say the town of Wiscasset — on the map with a gargantuan lobster roll that has seduced food critics and travel writers across the country and beyond. When he died in 2008, at the age of 71, his obituary appeared in newspapers from coast to coast. The *Los Angeles Times* proclaimed him "the lobster-roll king."

A master cook of unfussy, comforting foods, Gagnon added the lobster roll to his menu after sampling a disappointing version elsewhere. "I bit into it and — awg! — the frozen meat and what have you," a wincing Gagnon told WQED Pittsburgh's Rick Sebak in 2002. "I said to myself, 'You're going to make a lobster roll that's a *lobster roll*.'"

Gagnon's first effort mixed the seafood with a bit of mayonnaise, the most common preparation for lobster rolls in Maine. After hearing the words "hold the mayo" over and over, however, he took an ingeniously simple new tack: he stuffed his buns with an ultra-generous serving of unadorned lobster, and offered mayonnaise and drawn butter on the side. "People loved that," says cook Cindy Collamore, Gagnon's daughter, who is carrying on her father's legacy with sister Debbie Gagnon and brothers David and Joe Gagnon.

Indeed they did. Word of the mouthwatering mountain of goodness spread, enchanting vacationers, whose hordes attracted the attention of food and travel writers, whose rhapsodizing drew morning show hosts and television chefs, whose delirium called forth ever more vacationers. If you want to join them in their pursuit of the world's most famous lobster roll, be prepared to wait: in high summer, it can take more than an hour to work your way to the front of the line.

The Elements

The Bun: lightly buttered, griddled, split-top hot-dog rolls

The Meat: freshly cooked lobster delivered daily from local shellfish processors

The Mix: extra-heavy mayo, drawn butter, or both, served on the side

The Scene: the bank of the Sheepscot River in historic Wiscasset Village

Wharf Gallery & Grill

13 Gibbs Lane, Corea. 207-963-8888. corealunch.com

Retired lobsterman Joe Young has great admiration for his aunt, the late Louise Young, a distinguished photographer who documented life in mid-20th-century Corea, the fishing village where the Young family roots stretch to 1812. Louise was talented: She headed up the darkroom for Boston's venerable Bachrach Studios, and she worked for Berenice Abbott, making prints. Louise also was brave: "She was gay," Young explains, "and that was not easy in the forties and fifties. She was fierce and tenacious."

After Louise died at age 85, in 2004, Young honored her by opening a gallery in his fish house on Corea Harbor, where he showcases her work. "I'd come in from a haul, go down to the gallery and open it up, then sit and read a book," he says. "Occasionally, someone would stop in. Once in a while, someone would buy a print."

After the first couple of seasons, Young, at his wife's urging, set up a hot-dog cart to lure more people into the gallery. The next season, he added sausage sandwiches, and the next, lobster rolls. As the number of customers grew, he embraced what he calls his "accidental" career as a restaurateur and built a full kitchen, expanded the wharf, and added seating. Young's menu now includes fish chowder, steamed lobster dinners, crab claws, and lobster grilled cheese.

Most people, though, come for lobster rolls. From their perch on the wharf, they look across the harbor to the Corea Lobster Co-Op, where every morning Young buys a few crates of lobsters, which he then cooks for that day's sandwiches. Before or after they eat, customers usually step inside the gallery to catch a glimpse of Louise Young's Corea, a place at once changed and familiar, and ever beautiful.

The Elements

The Bun: a classic New England split-top roll, grilled

The Meat: caught by local lobstermen and cooked in salted water

The Mix: a touch of Hellmann's and a little pepper

The Scene: lobsterboats and wharves stacked with lobster traps — and an art gallery in a fish house

CHAPTER 3

Rolling in Lobsters

T'S A WARM afternoon in August, and you're sitting on the patio at Quoddy Bay Lobster in Eastport, getting ready to attack the jumbo lobster roll sitting on the table in front of you. But wait! Do you know how it got here? Yes, we know you picked up your *sandwich* at the take-out window, in all likelihood from manager Sara Griffin, but where did the *lobster meat* inside it come from?

60

To answer that question, we're going to deconstruct your roll and rewind its journey from takeout window to the sea.

Minutes before your sandwich emerged from the kitchen in its paper food tray, the day's cook — most likely Katie Johnson — was assembling it on the sandwich prep table, while also tending to scallops, haddock, and hot dogs browning on the grill. The prep table is like a refrigerated desk, each if its drawers filled with chunks of lobster, some mixed with mayo, some with Miracle Whip, and some plain. Dipping her gloved hand into whichever mix you ordered, Katie grabbed pieces of lobster — about 8 ounces for your jumbo — and stuffed them into a grilled 8-inch-long split-top bun. Katie finished her creation with a flourish — two whole claws laid atop the big roll.

The lobster meat that Katie piled onto your bun was picked from cooked lobsters that morning by Sharon Lucas. Yesterday, those lobsters were very much alive, crawling around in Quoddy Bay's holding tanks until Sara Griffin's husband, Brent, unbanded their claws and dropped them, along with 125 or so other "bugs," into steamer baskets, which he then lowered into a cook tank. Twenty minutes or so later, Brent rinsed the cooked lobsters and deposited them into bus boxes to cool.

Brent owns Quoddy Bay Lobster with his dad and uncles, and odds

Steaming kettles of lobsters, like this one at Trenton Bridge Lobster Pound, are such a common sight Down East that it's hard to imagine what the coast would look like without them.

are good that it was he who caught your lobsters the very same day that he steamed them. He's one of about a dozen lobstermen who deliver their daily catches to Quoddy Bay Lobster's wholesale operation next door on the pier.

Brent and his sternmen, Shane Griffin and Jeremy Brown, met on the dock at 4 that morning to load totes of ripe-smelling bait — salted herring, redfish, or pogies — onto the deck of Brent's 48-foot lobsterboat, *Triple Trouble*, named

for Brent and Sara's kids Natcha, Kyle, and Brett. By 4:45, *Triple Trouble* was motoring out to Brent's first green, white, and orange buoy, about an hour's voyage. The balloon-like polyball, used in offshore fishing instead of the more familiar bullet-shaped buoy, was tethered to a trawl, or line, of 15 cage-wire traps, each one weighted, baited, and resting on the ocean floor. Standing near the bow, Brent snagged the buoy with a gaff and winched the traps onto the gunwale. The three men worked quickly in tandem: Shane cleaned everything out of the first trap, throwing crabs and other fish overboard and handing the lobsters to Brent, who measured them and banded the claws of the keepers — lobsters that measure between 3.25 and 5 inches from their eye sockets to the edge of the carapace (body) — and tossed the shorts back into the sea. If there was a berried, or egg-bearing, female in the mix, he notched a V into her tail, a signal to any other fishermen who catch her that she's a fertile female and

The largest lobster ever caught weighed 44 pounds, 6 ounces, and was between 3 and 4 feet long, according to the *Guiness Book of World Records*. It was caught off Nova Scotia in 1977.

cannot be kept, and then he threw her overboard too. Shane slid the trap along the gunwale to Jeremy, who re-baited it and set it on the deck, as Shane and Brent worked the next one. Once the entire trawl was emptied and baited, it was dropped back into the sea, one trap after another. *Triple Trouble* moved on to the next green, white, and orange ball. By 3, Brent and his crew had delivered the contents of 400 traps to Quoddy Bay, where they were launched on the journey to your lobster roll.

THE LOBSTER CAPITAL OF THE WORLD

That's pretty much the way *Homarus americanus* — American lobster — is fished from New Jersey to Labrador, but lobstering takes on iconic status only in Maine, where the paraphernalia involved in catching, cooking, and serving the crustaceans is deeply interwoven into the sights and sounds of the coast. Consider: A stroll down Main Street in a coastal village of any consequence between Kittery and Eastport finds restaurants serving lobster steamed, stewed, ladled atop pasta, and stuffed into rolls. Lobsters find their way into paintings on art gallery walls, and their claws, rendered in 18-carat gold, clasp diamonds in jewelry store windows. Amble down any of Maine's peninsulas, where most of the state's 7,000 licensed lobstermen live, and you'll encounter traps stacked high in yard after yard.

The farther Down East you go, the more likely you are to find harbors like Port Clyde, which is primarily dedicated to commercial fishing, not pleasure boating.

Weathered bait sheds sit atop piers stretching into harbors dotted with lobsterboats — unless, of course, the lobstermen are out fishing, in which case you see them offshore, moving from buoy to buoy and pulling traps under a cloud of darting seagulls.

Lobsters account for 45 percent of all commercial landings in Maine (next, at 26 percent, is Atlantic herring — lobster bait). The Lobster Institute at University of Maine estimates the fishery's total economic impact on the state — from lobstermen and bait suppliers to dealers and processors to restaurants, stores, and marinas — to be as much as $1.7 billion.

Maine lobster's transition from luxury item to takeout treat parallels the growth of the lobster fishery during the early 2000s, when new landing records were broken every year. The abundant supply peaked in 2016, when 130 million pounds of lobster valued at $533 million were harvested. Even with a decrease in 2017, Maine still accounts for nearly 90 percent of the lobster landings in the Northeast.

CHAPTER 4

DIY Lobster Rolls
& Accompaniments

Lobster rolls are mainly a restaurant treat: one of the best things about them is that someone has done all the preliminary work of cooking and picking the lobster for you. But if you don't live in Maine, you may be hard pressed to find a place that makes a good one. And if you do live in Maine, you may have a difficult time finding one in the off-season. If this is your dilemma or, for that matter, if you like to cook and aren't daunted by live lobsters, then you may want to try making your own lobster rolls. Here are several ways to satisfy your cravings.

Steamed Lobster

You can't make a lobster roll without lobster meat. We prefer to steam lobsters because boiling tends to result in slightly watery lobster meat.

Live 1–1½-pound lobsters, one for each roll

Choose a kettle large enough to hold all your lobsters and add 2 inches of seawater or salted tap water (about 1 tablespoon sea salt per quart). Place a steamer rack in the pot, and bring the water to a rolling boil. Place lobsters in the pot and cover tightly. Start timing when the water returns to a boil

— about 10 minutes for 1-pound soft-shell lobsters and 12 minutes for 1-pound hard-shell lobsters. Add 1–2 minutes for each additional quarter–pound. Lift the cooked lobsters out with tongs and let drain in a colander for a few minutes. They're ready to pick when they're cool enough to touch.

About soft-shell and hard-shell lobsters: Soft-shells lobsters have molted recently and have grown into new, larger shells. Because they're soft, these shells are easier to crack. Soft-shells have less meat per pound than hard-shells, but many people say the meat is more tender and sweet. Soft-shell lobsters don't ship well, so if you're buying your lobsters outside of New England, they're almost certainly hard-shells.

Chef Sam Hayward's Classic Lobster Roll

Sam Hayward, the James Beard Award–winning chef of Portland's Fore Street and Scales restaurants, developed this crustacean creation for his first iteration of Scales, which was located in the Portland Public Market.

Four 1½-pound lobsters, slightly undercooked, chilled, and picked

4 split-top New England hot-dog rolls*

*Ours were made by Standard Baking Co. They succeeded in replicating the soft, fine crumb and texture of commercial renditions, but without any extraneous ingredients like dough conditioners or corn syrup.

Freshly milled black pepper

- Cut the lobster tails into ½- to ¾-inch pieces. Leave the knuckles and claw meat intact.

- Pre-heat a griddle or cast-iron skillet large enough to contain the rolls. Spread soft butter on the sides of the rolls and toast them until golden and slightly crisp.

- In a non-reacting skillet over moderate heat, melt the remaining butter until it begins to foam. Reduce the heat slightly, add the lobster meat, and toss to coat lightly with the butter. Continue cooking and tossing about two minutes, or until the lobster pieces are gently warmed throughout, avoiding overcooking.

- Immediately divide the lobster meat among the rolls. Sprinkle a little coarse Maine sea salt over the lobster meat, followed by the pepper and a scattering of sliced chives. Serve warm, and pass the mayo separately.

Coarse Maine
sea salt

4 ounces
unsalted butter

2 teaspoons
fresh chives,
sliced finely

Mayonnaise, ideally
homemade, to taste*

*At Scales, we made a gentle mayo with
a fine corn oil substituting for olive oil. We
tarted it up with fresh lemon and seasoned
with sea salt and a pinch of cayenne.

Bite Into Maine Picnic-Style Lobster Roll

1 cup mayonnaise, preferably extra-heavy

½ cup apple cider vinegar

¼ cup sugar

½ teaspoon salt

½ teaspoon pepper

half a medium head green cabbage, thinly sliced

half a medium head red cabbage, thinly sliced

1 carrot, shredded

4 split-top New England–style hot-dog buns

1 cup (1 stick) salted butter, melted

1½ pounds fresh Maine lobster, cooked and chilled

celery salt

half a lemon, cut into 4 wedges

In large bowl, whisk mayonnaise, vinegar, sugar, salt, and pepper. Add cabbage and carrot. Toss to coat. Chill.

Heat a skillet or griddle over medium-high heat. Using a pastry brush, liberally brush the melted butter on both sides of the hot-dog rolls and place in the skillet. Toast each side to a golden brown color, using more butter as needed.

For each roll, add a layer of coleslaw on the bottom, filling one-quarter to half-way.

Divide the lobster between each roll. Sprinkle with a dash of celery salt. Finish by pouring remainder of melted butter over the top to your liking. Serve with lemon wedges, which also can be squeezed on top.

Serve immediately, preferably with a water view.

Yardbird Canteen's Spicy Mayo Lobster Roll

Chef Michael Mastronardi elevates seafood shack fare at Yardbird Canteen in Tenants Harbor. Here's his spin on the classic lobster roll. Serves one.

- 1½-pound Maine lobster, preferably soft-shell, steamed and picked
- 2 tablespoons mayonnaise, preferably Japanese (see note), but Hellmann's will work well
- 1 tablespoon Sriracha hot sauce
- 1 split-top New England–style hot-dog bun or brioche sandwich roll
- 1 tablespoon butter
- chopped scallions for garnish

In a small bowl, combine the mayo and Sriracha, and mix well. Tear the meat into large chunks. Combine with just enough mayo to coat. Melt butter in a pan on medium heat. Once the butter stops bubbling, add your roll and toast on both sides. Fill the roll with lobster mix, top with scallions, and enjoy.

A WORD ON MAYONNAISE

Several of the recipes in this book call for extra-heavy mayonnaise. Sold primarily to the food-service industry, extra-heavy mayonnaise has a higher egg content than regular mayonnaise, yielding a rich taste and ultra-creamy consistency. You can buy it online, but be prepared to make a lot of sandwiches: it comes in nothing smaller than a one-gallon jar.

Note: Japanese mayo is yellower, creamier, and slightly tangier and sweeter than standard American mayo, thanks to ingredients like egg yolks (instead of whole eggs) and apple or rice vinegar (instead of distilled white vinegar). Find it at Asian markets, in the Asian foods aisle of some supermarkets, and online.

- -

Yardbird Canteen's Haddock Chowder

Mastronardi's fondness for homestyle cooking comes through in this rich, classic haddock chowder. Serves four.

- 2 tablespoons butter
- 1 large white onion, medium dice
- 2 stalks celery, medium dice
- 1 large shallot, sliced
- 1 bunch scallions, small dice, plus more for garnish
- ½ cup dry white wine
- 2 large Yukon Gold potatoes, skin on, large dice
- 1½ cups heavy cream
- 1½ cups whole milk
- salt and freshly ground pepper, to taste
- pinch sugar
- 1½ pounds fresh haddock, cut into 2-inch chunks

Set a large pot over medium-high heat. Add butter, onion, and celery. Cook for 6 minutes or until softened and translucent, stirring frequently. Add shallots and scallions, and cook for another 3–5 minutes, stirring frequently. Add the white wine and simmer until it's reduced and almost evaporated, 3–5 minutes. Add potatoes, and cover with the cream and milk. Additional cream or milk may be needed depending on the consistency you like. Bring to a slight boil and reduce heat to a simmer, stirring every couple of minutes. Cook until the potatoes are tender, 10–15 minutes. Season to your liking with salt, freshly ground black pepper, and a pinch of sugar. Fold in your haddock and cook gently until it is cooked through, about 5 minutes. Serve topped with freshly chopped scallions and crusty bread.

THE QUINTESSENTIAL LOBSTER ROLL BUN

Classic Maine lobster rolls are served on New England–style hot-dog buns. These are split-top, or top-loading, rolls with flat sides for a great grilling surface and a flat bottom so they stand up without tipping over. According to the *Boston Globe*, New England–based bakery J.J. Nissen created the roll for the Howard Johnson's restaurant chain. If you are unable to find them in your area, try using another roll and slice the sides flat for a greater grilling surface.

Almost-Like-Eventide's Lobster Roll

Yearning for an Eventide lobster roll, but you're not going to be in Portland for a while? Here's a

1 tablespoon fresh lemon juice

sea salt, to taste

8 frozen bao bao (Asian-style steamed buns) (see note)

finely chopped chives, for garnish

Steam buns according to package directions. Melt butter in a medium skillet over medium heat until its solids begin to brown and smell nutty. Add lobster meat, lemon juice, and salt, and cook until seafood is heated through, about 5 minutes. Divide lobster between buns and top with chives. Serve immediately.

Note: Wiley says you can also make your own buns using a Parker House rolls recipe; just steam instead of bake.

- -

Red's Eats' Legendary Lobster Roll

The world's most famous lobster roll is also the simplest. Makes one roll.

1 split-top hot-dog bun, sides brushed with melted butter

freshly cooked meat picked from one 1- to 1½-pound Maine lobster, including two whole claws and a whole tail, deveined and split

drawn butter, optional

mayonnaise, preferably extra-heavy, optional

Eventide's lobster roll was inspired by Asian steamed pork buns, a popular bar snack at sister restaurant Hugo's.

cheater substitute using frozen Asian buns. Eventide chef Mike Wiley says it won't be as good as the real thing, but it might satisfy your craving — at least for a little while. Makes 8 rolls.

8 tablespoons unsalted butter

1 pound Maine lobster meat, slightly undercooked, hand-torn into bite-size pieces

Grill the hot-dog bun until sides are toasted and golden. Rip lobster meat into chunks and fill the middle of the roll. Put the whole claws at each end of the roll and put the split lobster tail on top. Eat as is or drizzle with drawn butter or mayonnaise.

Red's Eats' Coleslaw

Al Gagnon, who put the little red Wiscasset food stand on the map, was an intuitive chef who relied on sight and taste, not measuring cups, to make delicious food. The cooks at Red's Eats have preserved his approach, as this coleslaw recipe attests.

- **cabbage, shredded**
- **carrots, shredded**
- **mayonnaise, preferably extra-heavy**
- **sugar, to taste**
- **apple cider vinegar, to taste**

Stir together shredded cabbage and carrots. Add extra-heavy mayonnaise to desired consistency. Add a little sugar and apple cider vinegar. Taste. Adjust ingredients until it tastes the way you like it.

Cafe Miranda's Lobster Roll

Chef Kerry Altiero's Cafe Miranda restaurant in Rockland is known for its enormous menu and boldly flavored meals. Here, the 2012 Maine Lobster Chef of the Year shares his recipe for Miranda's deliciously garlicky lobster "roll." Reprinted with permission from *Adventures in Comfort Food* by Kerry Altiero and Katherine Gaudet (Page Street Publishing, Salem, MA; 2014).

- **3½ ounces cooked lobster meat**
- **1 tablespoon fresh parsley, chopped coarsely**
- **3 tablespoons aioli (recipe follows)**
- **chunk of focaccia, about 6 inches long and 3½ inches wide (see note)**
- **1 leaf romaine**
- **½ small tomato, sliced**

Place the lobster, parsley, and aioli in a bowl. Mix well. Split open focaccia to make room for the lobster, leaving the edge crust intact. Line the focaccia with the romaine. Put in the lobster, with the sliced tomato on top.

To make aioli: Place 2 large egg yolks, 3–4 garlic cloves, and 1 teaspoon freshly squeezed lemon juice in a blender. Blend until smooth. With blender running, very slowly pour in ½ cup good olive oil or a neutral

A garlicky home-
made aioli and
crusty fresh focaccia
set Cafe Miranda's
lobster roll apart.

vegetable oil. Blend until emulsified. Makes about ¾ cup. This will keep for weeks in your refrigerator.

About the focaccia: Altiero makes a sinfully delicious loaf at Cafe Miranda. You can find his recipe in *Adventures in Comfort Food*.

Sandy Oliver's Slightly Enhanced Lobster Salad

When friends visit food historian and cookbook author Sandy Oliver at her home on Islesboro, she often treats them to this delicious lobster salad, served on a bed of shredded lettuce. Leave out the orecchiette and scoop it into buttered and grilled split-top buns, and you have a fine, nearly classic lobster roll. Makes six servings.

- 3–4 Maine lobsters, cooked and picked
- 3 big handfuls of orechiette or small pasta of your choice, cooked until al dente, drained, and rinsed in cold water
- 1 shallot, finely chopped
- 2 ribs celery, finely chopped
- dollop mayonnaise, to taste
- salt and pepper

Mix all the ingredients together, toss until well blended, serve on a bed of lettuce.

Curried Mayonnaise

Sandy Oliver says this curried mayonnaise works for all kinds of shellfish like lobster, shrimp, and scallops, and for chicken or egg salad as well. Make a batch and keep it in the fridge for whenever you might use mayonnaise. It's perfectly good for a slightly different take on lobster rolls. Makes 1½ cups.

- 2 tablespoons vegetable oil
- ½ small Spanish onion, finely diced
- 1 clove garlic, finely chopped
- 1½ tablespoons mild curry powder
- ½ cup water
- salt and pepper, to taste
- 1½ cups mayonnaise
- 1 fresh lime, zested and juiced

Heat the oil in a small sauté pan over medium heat. Add the onion and cook until soft, about 5 minutes. Add the garlic and cook for 30 seconds, then add the curry powder, salt, and pepper, and cook for 1 minute, stirring constantly. Add water and cook until mixture reduces and thickens. Transfer to a bowl and let cool slightly. Stir it into the mayonnaise and use right away or store in a jar in the fridge until needed.

Add the curried mayonnaise to picked lobster to taste, squeeze a little lime juice on it, and garnish with a little of the zest.

Baked Zucchini Chips

Down East magazine senior editor Virginia M. Wright recommends these as a light and flavorful alternative to potato chips. Makes eight servings. (Oh, who are we kidding? Two people will scarf these down in no time.)

> 4 large zucchinis
> olive oil spray
> salt, to taste
> smoked paprika, to taste
> ground cumin, to taste

Thinly slice the zucchini, preferably with a mandoline. Lay the zucchini slices on paper towels in a single layer. Cover with more paper towels and set a baking sheet on top of them. Press down on the baking sheet, applying slight pressure, to help squeeze out some of the moisture.

Preheat the oven to 225 degrees. Line a couple baking sheets with parchment paper and spray with olive oil. Lay the zucchini slices in a single layer on the parchment paper, spray with olive oil, and sprinkle with salt, paprika, and cumin.

Bake for 1½–2 hours until crisp and golden. If some zucchini chips are still a little soft or moist, remove the crisp chips and place the moist chips back in the oven for a few more minutes. Let the zucchini chips cool on the paper towels. Store in an air-tight container.

The Northwoods Gourmet Girl's Citrus Gin Fizz

Abby Freethy, who has been both a Lobster Chef of the Year judge and a finalist (she makes a killer grilled lobster sandwich), likes to serve this cool, light drink with lobster in any of its preparations. Chef Freethy is the owner of Northwoods Gourmet Girl, a maker of all-natural relishes, mustards, preserves, dessert sauces, and other pantry staples near Moosehead Lake in Greenville, Maine. Makes 1 cocktail, plus the ingredients for more.

> 1 cup white sugar
> 1 cup water
> 2 rosemary sprigs
> 1 lemon, preferably Meyer
> 1 jigger Hendrick's gin
> ¼ cup club soda
> 1 ounce (2 tablespoons) ruby grapefruit juice

Make the simple syrup: In a small saucepan, stir together sugar and water. Heat until the sugar is dissolved. Add one sprig of rosemary and let cool. Remove the rosemary (or leave it in if you want a stronger rosemary flavor).

Fill a martini glass with ice and water and set it aside to chill.

Fill a cocktail shaker with ice.

Zest the lemon with a micro-grater and reserve the zest. Roll the lemon to release its juices and cut it in half.

Squeeze the juice from one of the lemon halves into the shaker. Add a pinch of lemon zest, 1 jigger of gin, ¼ cup club soda, 2 tablespoons grapefruit juice, and 1 jigger of simple syrup. Cover and shake vigorously.

Roll a sprig of rosemary around the inside of your emptied, chilled glass to release its oils, and leave it in the glass as a garnish. Add fresh ice if you like and pour cocktail mix over top.

Luke's Lobster Blueberry Pie

Wild blueberries are smaller and have more complex flavor than their cultivated counterparts. Naturally growing stands of wild, or lowbush, blueberries are commercially harvested only in Maine and eastern Canada. Fresh ones are almost impossible to find in markets south of New England.

CRUST (yields 3 single crusts)
4 cups all-purpose flour
3 tablespoons granulated white sugar
2 teaspoons kosher salt
1¾ cups cold vegetable shortening

½ cup cold water
1 large egg, beaten
1 teaspoon demerara or turbinado sugar (for sprinkling on top)

FILLING
4½ cups Maine wild blueberries, fresh or frozen (but not thawed)
½ cup granulated white sugar
½ cup light brown sugar
2 tablespoons all-natural lemon juice
4 tablespoons all-purpose flour
½ teaspoon ground cinnamon
¼ teaspoon ground nutmeg
½ teaspoon kosher salt

GLAZE FOR CRUST
1 large egg, mixed with 1 tablespoon water

Heat oven to 350 degrees F.

In a large bowl, mix together the flour, granulated sugar, and kosher salt needed for the crust.

Add cold shortening to bowl and cut into dry ingredients using a fork, until mixture is pea-size lumps.

Mix together cold water and egg. Add to bowl and mix all ingredients until they come together in a loose ball.

Place dough onto floured surface and form into three disks. Cover each disk with plastic wrap and refrigerate for at least 30 minutes, or freeze for up

to 1 month. Only two disks will be needed for this recipe, so the third can be saved in freezer for a future tart.

Place chilled or thawed dough on floured counter, and use a rolling pin to make two circles, about $\frac{1}{16}$-inch thick.

Place 1 dough round over pie pan and press into sides. The second dough round will be the top of the pie. Chill the dough in fridge while you make the pie filling.

Combine filling ingredients in a large bowl and toss until blueberries are fully coated. Use fresh or frozen (not thawed) blueberries.

Add filling to pie dough, and place second pie dough over the filling. Press the edges together, cutting off excess dough, to seal the crust.

Brush egg wash over top of crust and sprinkle with demerara sugar. Using a paring knife, cut two small slits in center of crust to allow steam to escape.

Bake in oven for 1 hour 20 minutes, or until crust is golden brown. Let cool for at least 30 minutes before serving. Serve with ice cream and enjoy!

Bob's Clam Hut in Kittery produces a winning roll by sticking to tradition.

CHAPTER 5

The Lobster Roll Trail

We sampled Maine lobster rolls
from north to south and east to west.
These are our favorites.

During the high season, the wait can be up to an hour at The Clam Shack.

At this downtown Kennebunk gem (famous for its lobster pot pie), freshly made mayonnaise elevates tail, knuckle, and claw meat, and the bun is griddled in tasty sea-salt compound butter.

Kennebunkport

ADMIRAL'S TABLE
Rhumb Line Resort, 41 Turbats Creek Rd. 207-967-5457. rhumblineresort.com

You'll find fantastic lobster rolls off the beaten path at the Rhumb Line Resort's poolside tiki-ish bar.

Kittery

BOB'S CLAM HUT
315 U.S. Rte. 1. 207-439-4233. bobsclamhut.com

Bob's has us convinced that staying true to tradition is, more often than not, the way to go. This roll won the coveted Editors' Choice award at the Lobster Roll Rumble in New York City. See page 40.

ROBERT'S MAINE GRILL
326 U.S. Rte. 1. 207-439-0300. robertsmainegrill.com

Bob's sister restaurant takes the same straightforward approach to a classic roll: plenty of meat and a

SOUTHERN MAINE

Kennebunk

THE CLAM SHACK
2 Western Ave. 207-967-3321. theclamshack.net

On Lanigan's Bridge above the Kennebunk River, The Clam Shack has a reputation for piling fresh lobster meat (cooked in salt water) onto a round, toasted roll custom-made by a local bakery. It's served with the option for just mayo, just butter, or a little bit of both. This sandwich is a favorite of celebrities, from Al Roker to Barbara Bush. See page 42.

PEARL KENNEBUNK BEACH — SPAT OYSTER CELLAR
27 Western Ave. 207-204-0860. pearloysterbar.com

Chef Rebecca Charles didn't invent the lobster roll, but she does get a lot of credit for introducing it to the world via her Pearl Oyster Bar in Manhattan's West Village. Spat's lobster roll, like Pearl's, is decadent, mayo-heavy, and generous.

THE KENNEBUNK INN — ACADEME
45 Main St. 207-985-3351. thekennebunkinn.com

The Clam Shack's distinctive round bun is baked fresh daily at Reilly's Bakery in Biddeford.

Lobster rolls have sur-
passed fried clams in
popularity at Bob's
Clam Hut in Kittery.

A lobster roll and fries is served up with a breathtaking view at the Lobster Shack at Two Lights in Cape Elizabeth.

light touch of mayo. Get the regular or indulge and go for the jumbo.

Ogunquit

BARNACLE BILLY'S

50 Perkins Cove Rd.
207-646-5575.
barnbilly.com

Worth braving the summer traffic for this weighty roll — neatly dressed with mayo, loaded with meat, and dusted with paprika.

Old Orchard Beach

THE BRUNSWICK

39 W. Grand Ave. 207-934-4873.
thebrunswick.com

This classic OOB destination serves a delicious and overstuffed lobster roll with crinkle-cut fries that you can enjoy practically sitting on the beach.

Wells

BILLY'S CHOWDER HOUSE

216 Mile Rd. 207-646-7558.
billyschowderhouse.com

Billy's has a reputation for testing how much fresh, sweet lobster a bun can handle before splitting at the sides.

FISHERMAN'S CATCH

134 Harbor Rd. 207-646-8780.
fishermanscatchwells.com

This roll was a favorite of one of our testers, who found the meat to be dressed with just the right amount of mayo.

THE MAINE DINER

2265 Post Rd. 207-646-4441.
mainediner.com

It's all about "the Jim Nantz" — a combo meal of a hot or cold lobster roll and a side of mind-numbingly-good seafood chowder.

Multiple Locations
AMATO'S

amatos.com

Perhaps surprisingly, the chewy, pillowy rolls at the statewide Amato's chain make a terrific conduit for a generous heap of finely chopped lobster meat. Kennebunk: 48 Portland Rd.; 207-985-0014. Kittery: 103 U.S. Rte. 1 Bypass; 207-439-2168.

GREATER PORTLAND

Cape Elizabeth
BITE INTO MAINE

Food Truck, Fort Williams Park. 207-420-0294. biteintomaine.com

One of the best rolls on wheels, Bite Into Maine's sandwich is served six ways: Maine-style with mayo and chives; Connecticut-style with melted butter; Picnic-style roll with a layer of coleslaw; and with wasabi, curry, or chipotle mayos. See page 38.

LOBSTER SHACK AT TWO LIGHTS

225 Two Lights Rd. 207-799-1677.
lobstershacktwolights

New visitors to Maine shouldn't skip a trip to "The Shack," both to see what a real (and real simple) lobster roll tastes like AND to learn to fend off seagulls.

Falmouth
TOWN LANDING MARKET

269 Foreside Rd. 207-781-2128.
townlandingmarket.com

Town Landing's ¼-pound lobster roll is all killer, no filler. Strictly to go.

DOCKSIDE GRILL

215 Foreside Rd.
207-747-5274.
thedocksidegrill.com

Dressed with citrus aioli and local greens, this lobster roll is a bit upscale. Enjoy it on the patio, overlooking yacht-filled Falmouth Harbor.

It's butter or mayo — or both — at the Lobster Shack at Two Lights.

The lime mayo mix is a customer favorite at Highroller Lobster in Portland.

An iconic, dockside, BYOB lobster joint that piles the fresh lobster high — a must-stop for first-time visitors to the state.

Portland

BECKY'S DINER

390 Commercial St. 207-773-7070. beckysdiner.com

Becky's might be better known for blueberry pancakes, but there's no denying the comfort factor of their lobster roll, served with mayo on a griddled bun with a side of fries and slaw.

BENNY'S FAMOUS FRIED CLAMS

199 Commercial St. 207-774-2084. bennysfamousfriedclams.weebly.com

This ramshackle spot boasts waterfront views and a roll filled with meat picked from a whole chicken (one-pound) lobster.

BITE INTO MAINE

Allagash Brewing Co., 50 Industrial Way. biteintomaine.com

Silver Sue, Bite Into Maine's 1977 Airstream, serves the same six great sandwiches that its food truck made famous: Maine-style with mayo and chives; Connecticut-style with melted butter; Picnic-style roll with a layer of coleslaw; and

Freeport

HARRASEEKET INN

162 Main St. 207-865-9377. harraseeketinn.com

All tastes are accommodated by the "Real Maine Meal," featuring your choice of lobster roll (hot or cold, small or large, dressed or undressed) alongside a cup of lobster stew and a beer.

HARRASEEKET LUNCH AND LOBSTER

36 Main St., South Freeport. 207-865-4888. harraseeketlunchandlobster.com

with wasabi, curry, or chipotle mayos. See page 38.

EVENTIDE OYSTER CO.

86 Middle St. 207-774-8538. eventideoysterco.com

Even die-hard traditionalists surrender to Eventide's brown-butter vinaigrette on a soft, steamed, house-made roll. It's one of the smallest rolls on our list, but that doesn't make it any less satisfying. You'd be tempted to order more than one anyway. See page 44.

HIGHROLLER LOBSTER CO.

104 Exchange St. 207-536-1623. highrollerlobster.com

This popular little food cart has evolved into a storefront serving super-tasty rolls with choices like jalapeño or lime mayo, added bacon or avocado, and even Indian ghee (clarified butter). See page 48.

J'S OYSTER

5 Portland Pier. 207-772-4828. jsoysterportland.com

The regulars at this iconic Commercial Street dive come from all walks of life — and they all appreciate the massive chunks of lobster crammed into a split, buttered, and grilled roll.

BEET SALAD 12.
TONNATO · TROUT ROE · PISTACHIO
ROASTED TURNIPS 11.
CRANBERRY · VEGAN XO · TARRAGON
RAZOR CLAMS & CHIPS 14.
VINEGAR · PAPRIKA · LEMON SALT
RED SNAPPER 16.
PEANUT · CHILI OIL · DAIKONBUSHI
FRIED BRUSSELS 12.
CHILI GARLIC VINEGAR · CARROT · MINT
FRIED EGGS 12.
CRAB · TAMARIND · FISH SAUCE · SHALLOT

E

OXBOW 7.
DOMESTIC
LIQUID RIOT 6.
IRISH GOODBYE
MARSHALL WHARF 7.
ATTENUATOR
MAINE BEER CO. 7.
LUNCH
BUNKER 7.
MACHINE
ALLAGASH 8.
TRIPEL

Eventide has reimagined the seafood shack with a sophisticated menu.

MIYAKE

468 Fore St. 207-871-9170.
miyakerestaurants.com

Chef Masa Miyake interprets the
Maine classic in sushi roll form,
with a sesame wrapper, lobster
meat tossed with spicy mayo, and
tobiko garnish. Utter perfection, if
you don't mind unorthodoxy.

OLD PORT SEA GRILL & RAW BAR

93 Commercial St. 207-879-6100.
oldportseagrill.com

Some slightly non-traditional
elements — herbs and crisp lettuce
— complement the sweet meat in
this monster roll.

PORTLAND LOBSTER COMPANY

*180 Commercial St. 207-775-
2112. portlandlobstercompany.com*

Nothing beats taking in a concert
on the waterfront patio while
tearing up a roll made with meat
from a whole lobster, brushed with
warm, sweet butter.

SCALES

68 Commercial St. 207-805-0444.
scalesrestaurant.com

Tossed with butter and garnished
with mayo, the tasty roll at this
Portland hot spot is a formidable
best of both worlds.

Highroller Lobster
Company serves
lobster rolls and
other simple fare
with craft beer..

Bite Into Maine's offerings at the Lobster Roll World Championship.

Bayley's has a strong claim as the originator of the Maine lobster roll.

BITE INTO MAINE

The Commissary, 185 U.S. Rte. 1. 207-289-6142. biteintomaine.com

Bite Into Maine's brick-and-mortar location serves the same six great sandwiches that were made famous by its food truck: Maine-style with mayo and chives; Connecticut-style with melted butter; Picnic-style roll with a layer of coleslaw; and with wasabi, curry, or chipotle mayos.
See page 38.

KEN'S PLACE

207 Pine Point Rd. 207-883-6611.

Famous for their crumb- and batter-fried seafood, the sweet lobster, lightly dressed with mayo, is ultra-fresh — the kitchen breaks down a mountain of just-caught lobsters each day.

SUSAN'S FISH-N-CHIPS

1135 Forest Ave. 207-878-3240. susansfishnchips.com

An iconic Portland eatery in a former auto garage, Susan's roll is simple and classic (and for your fried seafood supplement, there are mason jars full of tartar sauce on every table).

Raymond
FISHERMEN'S CATCH

1270 Roosevelt Trl. 207-655-2244. fishermenscatchraymond.com

Customize your order and choose from three roll options and four lobster fillings, ranging from classic mayo to a sweet relish and mayo mixture.

Scarborough
BAYLEY'S LOBSTER POUND

9 Ave. 6. 207-883-4571. bayleys. com

A locals' favorite, known for oversized rolls made with lobster landed at their own docks,

Yarmouth
DAY'S CRABMEAT AND LOBSTER

1269 U.S. Rte. 1. 207-846-3436. dayscrabeatandlobster.com

One of the best lobster rolls in the state, always fresh, with a no-mayo option for the purists.

PAT'S PIZZA

791 U.S. Rte. 1. 207-846-3701.
patsyarmouth.com

A great seasonal value — no frills, but tasty — Pat's roll has mounds of chilled, freshly picked meat served on a toasted roll. Exclusive to the Yarmouth link in the Pat's chain.

Multiple Locations
AMATO'S

amatos.com

Perhaps surprisingly, the chewy, pillowy rolls at the statewide Amato's chain make a terrific conduit for a generous heap of finely chopped lobster meat. Biddeford: 458 Alfred St.; 207-286-2934. Freeport: 20 Bow St.; 207-865-9478. Gorham: 3 Main St.; 207-839-2511. North Windham: 727 Roosevelt Trail; 207-892-0160. Portland: 71 India St.; 207-773-1682. 312 St. John St.; 207-828-5978. 1379 Washington Ave.; 207-797-5514. Saco: 469 Main St.; 207-286-2377. Scarborough: 234 U.S. Rte. 1, Oak Hill; 207-883-2402. South Portland: 1108 Broadway; 207-767-5916. Maine Mall, 364 Maine Mall Rd.; 207-773-9100. Westbrook: 120 Main St.; 207-856-2120.

MIDCOAST

Belfast
YOUNG'S LOBSTER POUND

2 Fairview St. 207-338-1160.
youngslobsterpound.webs.com

The tradition here is BYOB, counter service, and picnic tables out back with views of Belfast Harbor. A hefty pile of lobster meat, dressed with a hint of mayo, is stuffed into a sesame-seed kaiser roll.

Boothbay Harbor
BOOTHBAY LOBSTER WHARF

97 Atlantic Ave. 207-633-4900.
boothbaylobsterwharf.com

This roll is impressive in size — one of our testers had a whole piece of tail in hers. You'll come for the lobster but stay for the view.

THE LOBSTER DOCK

49 Atlantic Ave. 207-633-7120.
thelobsterdock.com

Another destination that's as easy to reach by sea as by road, the Lobster Dock lets you choose hot (with butter) or cold (with mayo), and each is perfectly complemented by fried artichoke hearts.

Some of the best lobster rolls are found in unexpected places, like Libby's Market in Brunswick.

Lobstermen get an early start at Five Islands in Georgetown.

Brunswick

FRONTIER CAFE
14 Maine St. 207-725-5222.
explorefrontier.com
Lobster meat sautéed in butter and served on a toasted round brioche bun — so darn good!

LIBBY'S MARKET
42 Jordan Ave. 207-729-7277.
Libby's roll is substantial and delicious. The lobster is (gasp!) shredded, a welcome textural variation on the more typical chunky approach.

Camden

THE RHUMB LINE
59 Sea St. 207-230-8495.
rhumblinecamden.com
Packed with lobster meat, this roll is served with hand-cut fries and a front-row seat on the comings and goings of yachts and schooners in Camden Harbor.

Georgetown

FIVE ISLANDS LOBSTER CO.
1447 Five Islands Rd. 207-371-2990. fiveislandslobster.com
Go for the "Big Boy," with double the lobster meat piled onto Five Islands' delicious potato buns.

Luke's at Tenants Harbor shares its profits with the Tenants Harbor Fishermen's Co-op. Opposite: McLoons Lobster Shack.

New Harbor
SHAW'S FISH & LOBSTER WHARF RESTAURANT

*129 State Rte. 32
207-677-2200.*

An old-school lobster shack with a roll distinguished by just enough shredded iceberg lettuce for some crunch against a soft and buttery roll.

Phippsburg
SPINNEY'S RESTAURANT

*987 Popham Rd.
207-389-1122.
spinneysonpophambeach.com*

A great view and a generously sized roll filled with freshly picked lobster meat at this throwback shack near Popham Beach.

Rockland
THE BRASS COMPASS CAFE

*305 Main St. 207-596-5960.
thebrasscompasscafe.com*

Chef Lynn Archer's lobster roll is top-notch, but you may choose to up the ante with the famous double-decker lobster club sandwich that brought chef Bobby Flay to his knees on a lobster "throwdown."

CAFE MIRANDA

15 Oak St. 207-594-2034.
cafemiranda.com

Maine Lobster Chef of the Year Kerry Altiero mixes lobster with garlicky aioli and stuffs it into his addictive fresh focaccia. Can't wait for your next trip to Rockland? Make your own, page 74.

CLAWS

743 Main St. 207-596-5600.
clawsrocklandmaine.com

Claws overloads a buttery, toasted New England–style roll with freshly picked lobster meat, just a touch of Hellmann's, and a dusting of paprika. Order it with melted butter if you prefer.

Rockport
GRAFFAM BROS. SEAFOOD SHACK

211 Union St. 207-236-8391.
lobsterstogo.com

This roll is simple and fresh, and the grilled bun lends a nice crunch. Order a few to go and have a picnic at nearby Rockport Harbor.

South Harpswell
DOLPHIN MARINA & RESTAURANT

515 Basin Point Rd.

207-833-6000.
dolphinmarinaandrestaurant.com

Lightly dressed with mayo and served on a toasted bun, the freshness of the lobster speaks for itself. Go with an appetite: the fish chowder, served with blueberry muffin, is legendary.

South Thomaston
MCLOONS LOBSTER SHACK

315 Island Road. 207-593-1382.
mcloonslobster.com

While you enjoy your roll, you'll see the lobsters for tomorrow's meal being landed right next door. See page 52.

MUSSEL RIDGE MARKET

20 Island Rd. 207-466-9068.
musselridgemarket.com

Sandwich maker extraordinaire Malcolm Bedell serves up a bountiful roll with meat dressed with a touch of mayo and sprinkled with chives.

Tenants Harbor
LUKE'S AT TENANTS HARBOR

12 Commercial St., St. George. 207-691-3020. lukeslobster.com

The lobster roll that took New York by storm has come home to Maine

Lining up for lobster rolls and other seafood treats at Wharf Gallery & Grill in Corea.

(see page 50). We're partial to Luke's Trio: half-sized versions of the lobster, crab, and shrimp rolls.

YARDBIRD CANTEEN
686 Port Clyde Rd.
207-372-2068.
Chef Michael Mastronardi lends simple elegance to traditional seafood-shack fare. His lobster roll is served on a toasted, locally baked brioche bun. Order it naked or with warm butter, mayo, or corn. Try Mastronardi's recipe for a spicy-mayo lobster roll, page 71.

Vinalhaven
GREET'S EATS
West Main St. 207-863-2057.
Take the best things about Maine and funnel them into one dining experience: can't beat the scenery or the freshness of the lobster at Greet's. Declared Maine's best lobster roll by *Down East* magazine in 2014. See page 46.

Wiscasset
RED'S EATS
41 Water St. 207-882-6128.
redseatsmaine.com
The most famous lobster roll of them all (see page 56). Red's serves a whole lobster on every bun, offering it with a choice of mayo or melted butter on the side. Be prepared to wait: it can take an hour or more for you to make your way through the line.

SPRAGUE'S LOBSTER
22 Main St. 207-882-1236.
In the time it takes to reach the window at Red's, you can cross the street and consume about three of Sprague's buttery, delicious rolls, which are filled with lightly dressed fresh lobster.

Multiple Locatons
AMATO'S
amatos.com
Surprisingly, the chewy, pillowy rolls of the statewide Amato's chain make a terrific conduit for a generous heap of finely chopped lobster meat. Brunswick: 148 Pleasant St.; 207-729-5514. Bath: 111 Centre St.; 207-442-9600.

ACADIA AND ENVIRONS
Bar Harbor
SIDE STREET CAFE
49 Rodick St. 207-801-2591.
sidestreetbarharbor.com
For many, no trip to MDI is complete without a lobster roll from Side Street Cafe, loaded with fresh knuckle, claw, and tail and prepared with your choice of cold mayo or melted butter.

Bernard
THURSTON'S LOBSTER POUND
9 Thurston Rd. 207-244-7600.
thurstonforlobster.com
With fresh meat from the fleet of lobsterboats bobbing right outside (you can watch the lobsters being brought in), Thurston's offers both a standard-size roll as well as a super-size version meant to be eaten with a fork.

Brooksville
BAGADUCE LUNCH
145 Franks Flat Rd. 207-326-4197. facebook.com/bagaduce
In a riverside setting this picturesque, the roll needs no frills — just a golden, perfectly buttered roll filled with a mountain of tender lobster meat.

Corea
WHARF GALLERY & GRILL
13 Gibbs Ln. 207-963-8888.
corealunch.com
This shack on the water adds a little salt and pepper and a

It's hard to beat a summer afternoon on the deck at Wharf Gallery and Grill in Corea.

heaping helping of amazing Down East seaside views.

Cranberry Isles
Hitty's Café
Cranberry House, 163 Cranberry Rd., Great Cranberry Island. 207-244-7845.

Chef Cezar Ferreira mixes lobster with secret dressing. After you eat, hit the museum for a little local history.

Southwest Harbor
CHARLOTTE'S LEGENDARY LOBSTER POUND
Two locations: 465 Seawall Rd., 207-244-8021.
The Half Shell, 130 Shore Rd.
charlotteslegendarylobsters.com

Charlotte's brioche roll and sweet lobster meat are top notch (we recommend holding the lettuce). The other homemade goodies on the menu make it a must-stop.

Trenton
TRENTON BRIDGE LOBSTER POUND
1237 Bar Harbor Rd. 207-667-2977. trentonbridgelobster.com

In a refreshing throwback to the lobster roll's lunch-pail origins, Trenton serves its tasty "lobster sandwich" on sliced white bread with lettuce.

USA Today readers voted Bayview Takeout's lobster roll the best in New England.

DOWN EAST

Beals

BAYVIEW TAKEOUT
42 Bayview Dr. 207-497-3301.
Bayview's lobster roll tips the scales! The split-top buns are always grilled to perfection, lending a buttery crunch to a pile of sweet meat generously dressed with mayo. Voted Maine's best lobster roll by *USA Today* readers. See page 36.

Eastport

QUODDY BAY LOBSTER
7 Sea St. 207-853-6640.
This spot on the shore of Friar Roads is owned by lobstermen whose traps supply the meat for some of the freshest rolls you'll find in the state. Learn how they do it on page 60.

CENTRAL AND WESTERN MAINE

Auburn

MAC'S DOWNEAST SEAFOOD
894 Minot Ave. 207-777-5871. macsdowneastseafood
The "clear meat" lobster roll (as opposed to Mac's pre-mixed lobster salad roll, which has no tail meat) comes on a split-top bun or a bigger sub roll, both piled high, buttered, and grilled.

Augusta

THE RED BARN
455 Riverside Dr. 207-623-9485. theredbarnmaine.org
How hungry are you? Red Barn's foot-long lobster roll, stuffed with 28 ounces of claw meat, should satisfy your craving and then some. Too much? Downsize to the half-pounder. Save room for owner Laura Benedict's seafood stew.

Brewer

EAGLES NEST RESTAURANT
1016 N. Main St. 207-989-7635.
This roadside shack uses processed, packaged lobster, but locals crowd the place for lightly dressed whole-claw rolls that threaten to spill off the plate.

Oakland

THE GREEN SPOT
818 Kennedy Memorial Dr. 207-465-7242
The Green Spot gives the traditional lobster roll a kick with some chives. The perfectly grilled bun and sweet meat balance the flavors nicely. Plus, it's a gem of a market for a picnic pit stop.

Weld

KAWANHEE INN
12 Anne's Way. 207-585-2000. kawanheeinn.com
Who knew that you could find such a tasty lobster roll in Maine's western mountains? Kawanhee's lemon aioli is a nice touch. Enjoy it with a local microbrew on the porch overlooking beautiful Webb Lake.

Multiple Locations

AMATO'S
amatos.com
Perhaps surprisingly, the chewy, pillowy rolls at the statewide Amato's chain make a terrific conduit for a generous heap of finely chopped lobster meat. Auburn: 1813 Washington St. So.; 207-786-3736. Augusta: 34 Western Ave.; 207-620-1120. Bangor: 657 Broadway; 207-942-2929. Holden: 1024 Main Rd.; 207-843-0888. Manchester: 867 Western Ave.; 207-480-4038.

A whole claw adorns every Bayview Takeout lobster roll.

Wharf Gallery & Grill's deck is just across the harbor from the Corea Lobster Co-Op.